*Follow* THE DRINKING GOURD

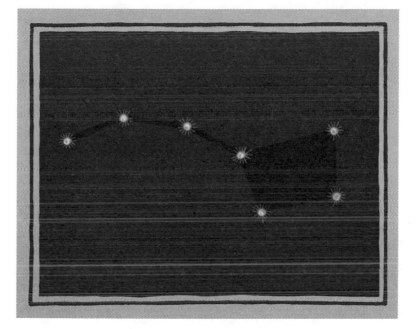

Story and Pictures by

JEANETTE WINTER

A TRUMPET CLUB SPECIAL EDITION

To Frances Foster

Published by The Trumpet Club
1540 Broadway, New York, New York 10036

Copyright © 1988 by Jeanette Winter

ISBN 0-440-84561-0

This edition published by arrangement with Alfred A. Knopf, Inc., a division of Random House, Inc.
Printed in the United States of America
January 1992

5 7 9 10 8 6 4
UPR

A NOTE ABOUT THE STORY

In the early days of slavery in the United States many slaves tried to escape their cruel bondage by fleeing north—usually to Canada—to freedom. By the 1840s a loosely organized group of free blacks, slaves, and white sympathizers formed a secret network of people and places that hid escaped slaves on their dangerous journey to freedom—a network that came to be known as the Underground Railroad.

Traveling along darkened roads at night, hiding out by day, moving slowly upriver along hundreds of miles of connecting waterways, the fugitive slaves endured many hardships. Slave catchers hunted them down with dogs. Many were shot or hanged. And even after crossing into the "free" states, runaway slaves could still be captured and returned to their masters for a reward.

One legendary conductor on the Underground Railroad was a one-legged sailor named Peg Leg Joe. Joe hired himself out to plantation owners as a handyman. Then he made friends with the slaves and taught them what seemed a harmless folk song—"Follow the Drinking Gourd." But hidden in the lyrics of the song were directions for following the Underground Railroad. The Drinking Gourd is the Big Dipper, which points to the North Star. "When the sun comes back, and the first quail calls" meant spring, when travel might be least hazardous. As the runaway slaves followed the stars north, they would come across marks Peg Leg Joe had made in mud or in charcoal on dead trees—a left foot and a peg foot—and they would know they were on the right trail.

The river that "ends between two hills" was the Tombigbee River. The second was the Tennessee River and the "great big river" was the Ohio River, where Peg Leg Joe would be waiting to ferry them across to the free states on the other side. From there the fugitives were guided from one hiding place to the next until—with luck—they made it to Canada or other safe places in the North.

L ong ago,
before the Civil War,
there was an old sailor called Peg Leg Joe
who did what he could to help free the slaves.

Joe had a plan.
He'd use hammer and nail and saw

and work for the master, the man
who owned slaves
on the cotton plantation.

Joe had a plan.
At night when work was done,
he'd teach the slaves a song
that secretly told the way
to freedom.
Just follow the drinking gourd, it said.

When the song was learned
and sung all day,
Peg Leg Joe would slip away
to work for another master
and teach the song again.

One day
a slave called Molly saw her man James
sold to another master.
James would be taken away,
their family torn apart.
Just one more night together.

A quail called in the trees that night.
Molly and James remembered Joe's song.
They sang it low.

> *When the sun comes back, and the first quail calls,*
> *Follow the drinking gourd.*
> *For the old man is a-waiting for to carry you to freedom*
> *If you follow the drinking gourd.*

They looked to the sky and saw the stars.

Taking their little son Isaiah,
old Hattie, and her grandson George,
Molly and James set out for freedom
that very night,
following the stars of the drinking gourd.

They ran all night through the fields,
till they crossed the stream to the woods.

When daylight came, they hid in the trees,
watching,
listening
for the master's hounds
set loose to find them.

But the dogs lost the runaways' scent
at the stream,
and Molly and James and Isaiah,
old Hattie and young George,
were not found.
They hid all day in the woods.

At night they walked again,
singing Joe's song
and looking for the signs
that marked the trail.

The riverbank makes a very good road,
The dead trees will show you the way.
Left foot, peg foot, traveling on,
Follow the drinking gourd.

Walking by night, sleeping by day,
for weeks they traveled on.
Sometimes berries to pick
and corn to snatch,
sometimes fish to catch,

sometimes empty bellies to sleep on.
Sometimes no stars to guide the way.

They never knew what lay ahead.

There was danger from men
who would send them back,
and danger from hungry beasts.
But sometimes a kind deed was done.

One day as they hid in a thicket
a boy from a farm found them.
In a bag of feed for the hogs in the wood
he brought bacon and corn bread to share.

Singing low, they traveled on.

The river ends between two hills,
Follow the drinking gourd.
There's another river on the other side,
Follow the drinking gourd.

On and on they followed the trail
to the river's end.
From the top of the hill they saw the new path,
another river beneath the stars
to lead them to freedom land.

The drinking gourd led them on.
The song was almost done.

When the great big river meets the little river,
Follow the drinking gourd.
For the old man is a-waiting for to carry you to freedom
If you follow the drinking gourd.

Then they climbed the last hill.
Down below was Peg Leg Joe
waiting at the wide Ohio River
to carry them across.

Their spirits rose when they saw the old man.
Molly and James and Isaiah, old Hattie and George,
ran to the shore.

Under a starry sky
Joe rowed them across the wide Ohio River.
He told them of hiding places
where they would be safe.
A path of houses stretched like a train
on a secret track leading north to Canada.
He called it the Underground Railroad.
It carried riders to freedom.

The first safe house stood on the hill.
The lamp was lit,
which meant it was safe to come.
Ragged and weary, they waited
while Joe signaled low, with a hoot like an owl.

Then the door opened wide
to welcome the freedom travelers.

They were rushed through the house
to the barn,
for the farmers knew
there were slave catchers near.

A trapdoor in the floor
took them under the barn,
to hide till it was safe to move on.
Then Peg Leg Joe went back to the river
to meet others who followed the drinking gourd.

With danger still near, too close for ease,
the farmer sent the five travelers on.
He drew a map that showed the way north
on the midnight road
to the next safe house, just over two hills.

This time James called the signal,
a hoot like an owl,
that opened the door to a Quaker farm.
The travelers were led to a secret room
hidden behind shelves.

They rested here for many days
and healed their wounds.
Soft beds, full meals, new clothes, hot baths,
washed away some fear and pain.
Isaiah smiled.

When they were strong, they traveled again
from house to house on the underground trail,
still following the drinking gourd north.

Sometimes they traveled on foot,
sometimes by cart.
The wagon they rode near their journey's end
carried fruit to market
and the runaways to freedom.

At last they came to the shores of Lake Erie.
Molly and James and Isaiah,
old Hattie and young George,
climbed aboard the steamship
that would carry them across
to Canada, to freedom.
"Five more souls are safe!"
old Hattie cried.
The sun shone bright when they stepped on land.

They had followed the drinking gourd.

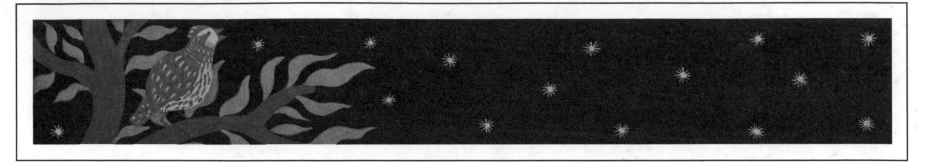

CHORUS

Fol - low _____ the drink - ing gourd! Fol - low _____ the

drink - ing gourd. _ For the old man is a - wait - ing for to

car - ry you to free-dom If you fol-low the drink - ing gourd. When the

VERSE

sun comes back, and the first quail calls, _ Fol - low _____ the

drink - ing gourd. _ For the old man is a - wait - ing for to

car - ry you to free-dom If you fol - low the drink - ing gourd.

(Repeat chorus)
The riverbank makes a very good road,
The dead trees will show you the way.
Left foot, peg foot, traveling on,
Follow the drinking gourd.

(Repeat chorus)
The river ends between two hills,
Follow the drinking gourd.
There's another river on the other side,
Follow the drinking gourd.

(Repeat chorus)
When the great big river meets the little river,
Follow the drinking gourd.
For the old man is a-waiting for to carry you to freedom
If you follow the drinking gourd.